WAY OF THE RAVEN

IMPACT WEAPONS COMBATIVES

SIDE HANDLE BATON VOLUME TWO

First Printing 2017

Raven Tactical International

Chicago, Illinois USA

www.RavenTactical.com

www.TheRavenTribe.com

www.FernanVargas.com

DEDICATION

This book is dedicated to friend, mentor and instructor Soke Joseph Truncale

Speak softly and carry a big stick; you will go far.

-Theodore Roosevelt

TABLE OF CONTENTS

ABOUT THE SYSTEM

ABOUT THE SYSTEM

The program is a multi-level program which trains individuals on a variety of impact weapons. The program teaches the Mini-baton, the Side Handle Baton, Riot Baton, Side Handle baton and more. This manual will specifically address the use of the Side Handle Baton for Self Defense. While it may be adapted to Peacekeeping personnel, all of the techniques presented here may not be suitable and should be evaluated by individual officer's employing department before adopting them for use..

The Program is not a stick fighting martial art such as Kali or Hanbo-Jutsu. The program is designed to be completed in a short period of time. The Program is meant to impart the student with "SURVIVAL ESSENTIALS". That is a minimum effective proficiency for self protection. This is not to say that the program is lacking in fact the program can be as functional and "Advanced" as the student wished it to be. Remember that "Advanced Material is the basics done well". Properly drilled and trained over time, this program can offer anyone a highly effective and reliable skill set for the use of the Side Handle Baton.

This program draws from numerous sources, including a variety of Police Baton methods, military baton methods, and select tactics from Stick Fighting Martial Arts or "Martial Baton Methods".

WHY THE SIDE HANDLE BATON?

T.J. Hooker. That's right T.J. Hooker is the reason that I wrote this book. It was not the "Shat" however that inspired me but Adrian Zmed. I remember being a small child in the 80's. I was watching an episode of T.J. Hooker where Adrian Zmed was working out in the police department gym. He was swinging and spinning this baton around. I had never seen a weapon like this one. As readers of my other books may know, 80's Television and movies were my instructors in my formative years, lol. There in all its glory was the coolest "Ninja Stick" that I had ever seen. Seed officially planted. Good job Adrian!!

As I grew in proper martial arts training I was exposed to the Tonfa again in my karate classes, and via dozens and dozens of martial arts books and magazines. When I began to learn Police defensive tactics I was introduced to the PR-24. It was like a Tonfa on steroids. I had seen the weapon used for striking and blocking but the PR-24 added a whole new dimension to training. Joint locks, come along holds, and takedowns now were taught to me.

The Tonfa and the PR-24 have fallen out of style in recent decades. This is a shame because the weapon still offers great versatility and impact. I firmly believe that the tonfa or Pr-24 still has a place among self defense minded individuals. A tonfa in the car or in the hall closet can be a valuable tool. In a world of firearms and knives, there are still people who shy away from poking and blowing holes in people. A good old fashioned bludgeon is a great alternative. A bludgeon that can be used in a variety of ways in a variety of grips is an even better one.

SHOULD THIS BOOK BE USED?

This book is primarily for the purpose of entertainment and information. There are those however who may wish to use it to train from. The book is not meant to be a training guide without the guidance of a qualified instructor. If anyone is interested in using the book as a training guide please contact me. I will connect you to a qualified instructor to guide you, or I will assist you myself.

SAFETY & USE OF FORCE

SAFETY IN TRAINING

Safety should be the paramount consideration during any training activity. We train so that we can protect ourselves and not get hurt. Why then would we allow being hurt in training? It is the responsibility of the instructor and all class participants to ensure the safety of all. All participants in a training activity should be led through a proper warm up and stretching routine before class begins.

SAFETY EQUIPMENT

Warriors should also use appropriate safety equipment for all training sessions. Equipment that should be used includes:

-Athletic Cup
-Athletic Mouth Piece
-Safety head gear
-Forearm shields
-Safety Goggles
-Safety Gloves

SAFETY TRAINING WEAPONS

Warriors should also use safe training weapons. A variety of training blades should be used from rubber to aluminum trainers. Dulled Live blades are inappropriate for anything but solo training purposes. NO LIVE WEAPONS SHOULD EVER BE ALLOWED IN THE TRAINING AREA. A good friend of mine was working in a seminar with another instructor. The Instructor drew his blade and cut my friend across the inside of his forearm as part of his demo. The only problem is that he drew his live blade and not a trainer. Luckily a few stitches were all that were needed that day. I shudder to think what would have happened if the instructor would have been demonstrating a neck cut?

OTHER CONSIDERATIONS

-Training should be conducted in reasonable proximity of emergency medical care

-Training should be conducted in a designated training area with adequate flooring, padding and ventilation.

SAMPLE FORCE CONTINUUM

SUBJECT ACTION	WARRIOR RESPONSE
Cooperation	**Verbal Commands**
Passive Resistance	**Escort Control**
Active Resistance	**Control & Compliance Holds**
Assault Which Can Result in Bodily Harm	**Defensive Tactics/Mechanical Controls/Less Lethal Weapons**
Assault Which Can Result In Serious Bodily Harm or Death	**Deadly Force**

**The use of force continuum presented is a general model based on common U.S. use of force guidelines. The continuum presented is for illustrative purposes only.*

FORCE CONTINUUM

The force continuum is a conceptual tool which exists to aid Warriors in determining what level of force is required and justified in controlling the actions of an assailant. Verbal commands, escort techniques, mechanical controls, and deadly force are all options which are available to an Warrior depending upon the assailant's actions. Force escalation must cease when the assailant complies with the commands of the Warrior, and/or the situation is controlled by the Warrior. The model presented bellow consists of five levels. Physical defensive tactics are appropriate from levels three to five.

Level One: The assailant cooperates with the Warrior's verbal commands. Physical actions are not required.

Level Two: The assailant is unresponsive to verbal commands. Assailant cooperation however is achieved with escort techniques.

Level Three: The assailant actively resists the Warrior's attempts to control without being assault. Compliance and control holds as well as pain compliance techniques are appropriate actions at this time.

Level Four: The assailant assaults an Warrior or another person with actions which are likely to cause bodily harm. Appropriate action would include mechanical controls or defensive tactics such as stunning techniques. Impact and chemical weapons may be appropriate at this level.

Level Five: The assailant assaults an Warrior or another person with actions which are likely to cause serious bodily harm or death if not stopped immediately. Appropriate Warrior action would include deadly force through mechanical controls, Impact weapons or firearms. Deadly force should be considered only when lesser means have been exhausted, are unavailable or cannot be reasonably employed.

DECISION OF FORCE

When making the decision to use force an Warrior should use the minimal amount of "Reasonable" force necessary to safely control the situation at hand. When using deadly force for self defense an Warrior must be prepared to articulate and justify their use of a force.

"Reasonable force" can be defined: *force that is not excessive and is the least amount of force that will permit safe control of the situation while still maintaining a level of safety for himself or herself and the public.*

A Warrior is justified in the use of force when they reasonably believe it to be necessary to defend themselves or another from bodily harm and have no avenue for reasonable escape.

Escalation and de-escalation of resistance and response may occur without going through each successive level. The Warrior has the option to escalate or disengage, repeat the technique, or escalate to any level at any time. However, the Warrior will need to justify any response to resistance. If the Warrior skips levels, he or she must explain why it was necessary to do so.

TOTALITY OF CIRCUMSTANCES

Totality of circumstances refers to all facts and circumstances known to the Warrior at the time. The totality of circumstances includes consideration of the assailant's form of resistance, all reasonably perceived factors that may have an effect on the situation, and the response options available to the Warrior.

SAMPLE FACTORS MAY INCLUDE THE FOLLOWING:

- Severity of the assault or battery
- Assailant is an immediate threat
- Assailant's mental or psychiatric history, if known to the Warrior
- Assailant's violent history, if known to the Warrior
- Assailant's combative skills
- Assailant's access to weapons
- Innocent bystanders who could be harmed
- Number of assailant's vs. number of Warriors
- Duration of confrontation
- Assailant's size, age, weight, and physical condition
- The Warrior's size, age, weight, physical condition, and defensive tactics expertise

- Environmental factors, such as physical terrain, weather conditions, etc.

In all cases where your assessment and decision are questioned you may need to demonstrate the following:

- That you felt physically threatened by and in danger from the suspect, i.e. that the suspect's behavior (body language/ words / actions) were aggressive and threatening;

- That you used force as a last resort, and that you used the reasonable amount;

- That you stopped using force once you had the suspect and the situation under control.

- That the Warrior has exhausted all reasonable efforts to escape the situation.

GRIPS, POSTURES & GUARDS

EXTENDED TONFA GRIP

To assume the tonfa grip, the warrior will hold the baton by the side handle, allowing for the shaft to run alongside the bottom of the warrior's forearm. The baton's pommel will extend outward past the closed fist.

REVERSE GRIP

To assume the reverse grip, the warrior will hold the baton by the sbottom part of the shaft close to the side handle, allowing for the shaft to run alongside the bottom of the warrior's forearm. The baton's pommel will extend outward past the closed fist.

TWO HANDED SWORD GRIP

The baton should be held in the strong hand. The baton should rest in the palm held firmly with a full grip as if you were holding a hammer. The second hand will grasp the remaining portion of the vertical grip. This grip allows for maximum range and powerful striking.

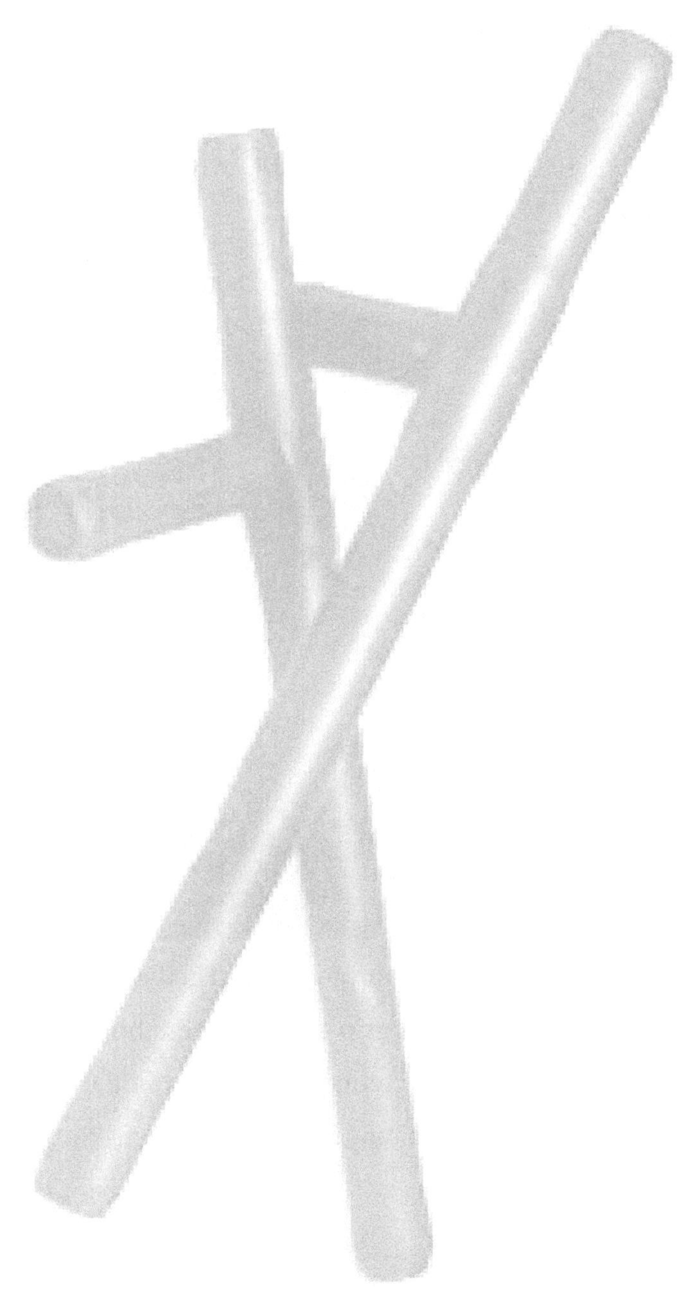

DEFENSIVE TECHNIQUES

LINES OF DEFENSE

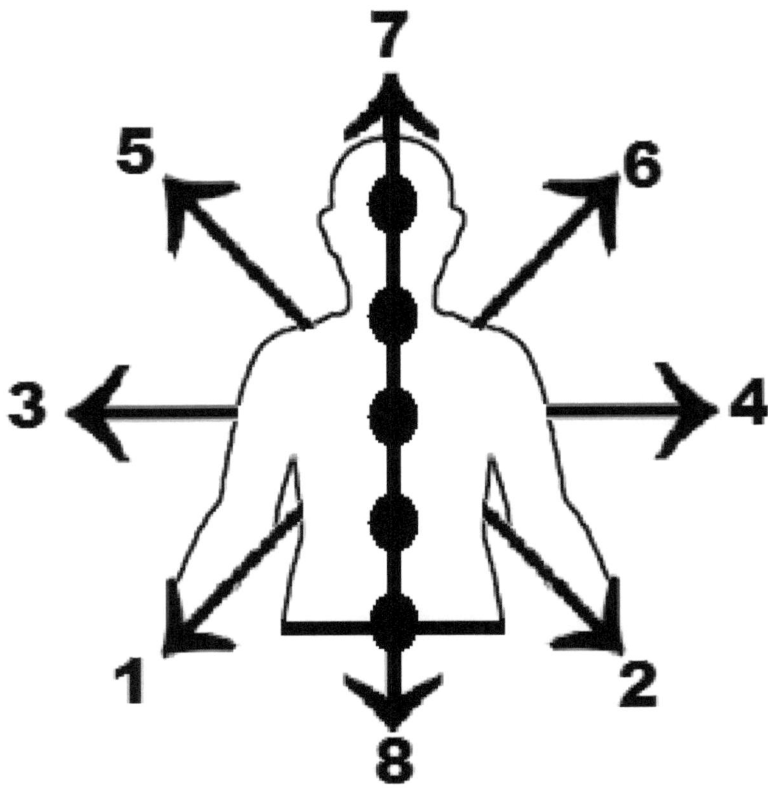

Blocking techniques will be executed on particular lines of interception. A direct thrust can come at any elevation on the vertical line. In addition to this attack virtually all other attacks will come on one of the 8 lines illustrated above. The most common angles of defense used are on the horizontal line, #3 &4 and on the vertical line, # 7& 8. A Warrior can make slight adjustments to adequately defend the diagonal lines in between. For this reason all illustrations and photos of defensive techniques in this book reflect the four fundamental lines of interception with the clear understanding that there are 8 lines in total, 4 primary and 4 secondary.

REVERSE GRIP HIGH BLOCK

A high block is executed against a vertical attack coming from high to low. Forcefully thrust your arms up at approximately a 45-degree angle from your body. The elbows are bent but there is enough muscular tension in the arms to absorb the impact and deter the attack.

REVERSE GRIP DOWNWARD BLOCK

The low block is executed against a vertical attack coming from low to high. Forcefully thrust your arms down at approximately a 45-degree angle from your body. The elbows are bent but there is enough muscular tension in the arms to absorb the impact and deter the attack.

Reverse Grip Inside Block

The inside block is executed against a linear or circular attack coming toward the Warrior. Forcefully sweep the arm in front of the body from outside of the body to the inside of the body across the center line. The arm is held at a 45 degree angle. The elbows are bent but there is enough muscular tension in the arms to absorb the impact and deter the attack.

Reverse Grip Outside Block

The Outside block is executed against a linear or circular attack coming toward the Warrior. Forcefully thrust the forearm outwards towards the attack from the inside of the body to the outside of the body. The Warriors hand should not cross much farther than the shoulder. The arm is held at a 45 degree angle. The elbows are bent but there is enough muscular tension in the arms to absorb the impact and deter the attack.

REVERSE GRIP INSIDE SWEEPING BLOCK

The inside sweeping block is executed against a linear or circular attack coming toward the Warrior. Forcefully sweep the baton in front of the body from outside of the body to the inside of the body across the center line. The warrior should step back to further avoid the attack.

OUTSIDE SWEEPING BLOCK

The outside sweeping block is executed against a linear or circular attack coming toward the Warrior. Forcefully sweep the baton in front of the body from inside of the body to the outside of the body across the center line. The warrior should step back to further avoid the attack.

EXTENDED GRIP
HIGH BLOCK

A high block is executed against a vertical attack coming from high to low. Forcefully thrust your arms up at approximately a 45-degree angle from your body. The elbows are bent but there is enough muscular tension in the arms to absorb the impact and deter the attack.

EXTENDED GRIP
DOWNWARD BLOCK

The low block is executed against a vertical attack coming from low to high. Forcefully thrust your arms down at approximately a 45-degree angle from your body. The elbows are bent but there is enough muscular tension in the arms to absorb the impact and deter the attack.

EXTENDED BLOCK INSIDE BLOCK

The inside block is executed against a linear or circular attack coming toward the Warrior. Forcefully sweep the arm in front of the body from outside of the body to the inside of the body across the center line. The arm is held at a 45 degree angle. The elbows are bent but there is enough muscular tension in the arms to absorb the impact and deter the attack.

EXTENDED GRIP OUTSIDE BLOCK

The Outside block is executed against a linear or circular attack coming toward the Warrior. Forcefully thrust the forearm outwards towards the attack from the inside of the body to the outside of the body. The Warriors hand should not cross much farther than the shoulder. The arm is held at a 45 degree angle. The elbows are bent but there is enough muscular tension in the arms to absorb the impact and deter the attack.

SWORD GRIP HIGH BLOCK

A high block is executed against a vertical attack coming from high to low. Forcefully thrust your arms up at approximately a 45-degree angle from your body. The elbows are bent but there is enough muscular tension in the arms to absorb the impact and deter the attack.

SWORD GRIP DOWNWARD BLOCK

The low block is executed against a vertical attack coming from low to high. Forcefully thrust your arms down at approximately a 90-degree angle from your body. The elbows are bent but there is enough muscular tension in the arms to absorb the impact and deter the attack.

SWORD GRIP INSIDE BLOCK

The inside block is executed against a linear or circular attack coming toward the Warrior. Forcefully sweep the arm in front of the body from outside of the body to the inside of the body across the center line. The arm is held at a 45 degree angle. The elbows are bent but there is enough muscular tension in the arms to absorb the impact and deter the attack.

SWORD GRIP OUTSIDE BLOCK

The Outside block is executed against a linear or circular attack coming toward the Warrior. Forcefully thrust the forearm outwards towards the attack from the inside of the body to the outside of the body. The Warriors hand should not cross much farther than the shoulder. The arm is held at a 45 degree angle. The elbows are bent but there is enough muscular tension in the arms to absorb the impact and deter the attack.

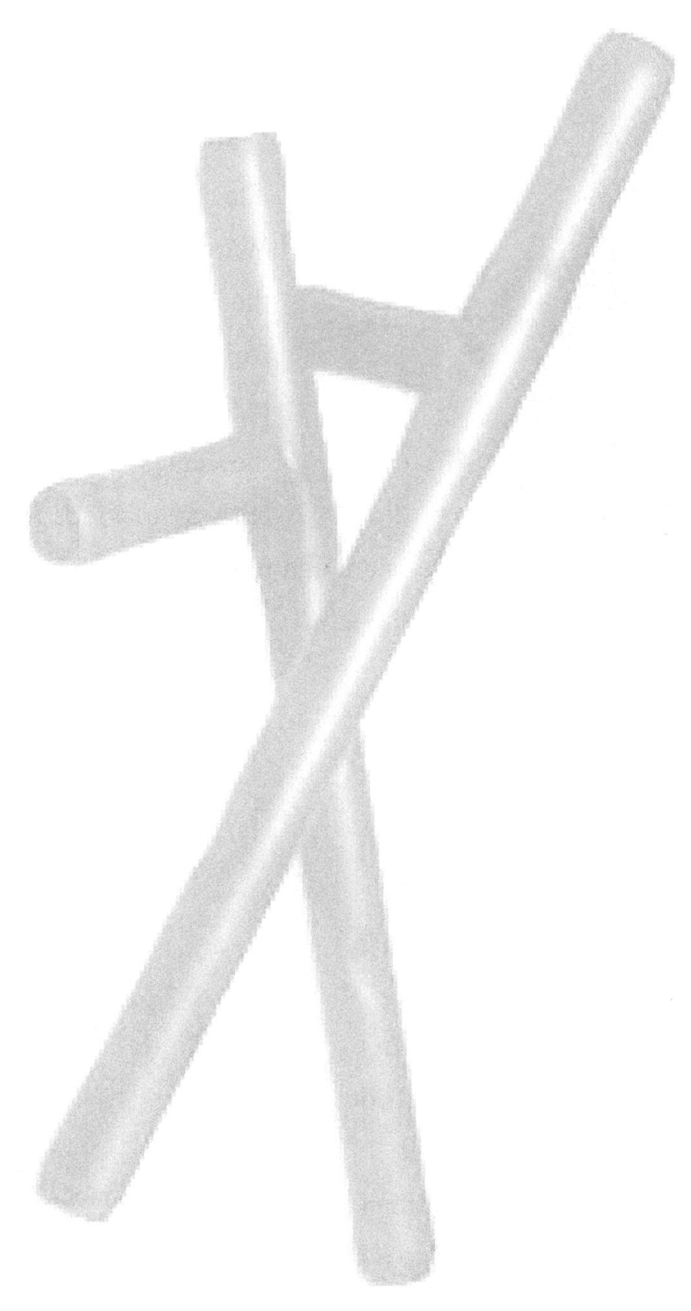

STRIKING TARGETS

CONFLICT ANATOMY

The basic study of human anatomy is essential to Defensive Tactics training. The information acquired is important in two respects. First Warriors must be aware of the vulnerable points of the body in order to better protect themselves from assaults by others. Secondly, Warriors must be conscience of what effects their counter measures and mechanical controls will have on a subject. Use of inappropriate force by an Warrior can quickly become a tragedy for all involved.

POINTS OF THE HUMAN BODY

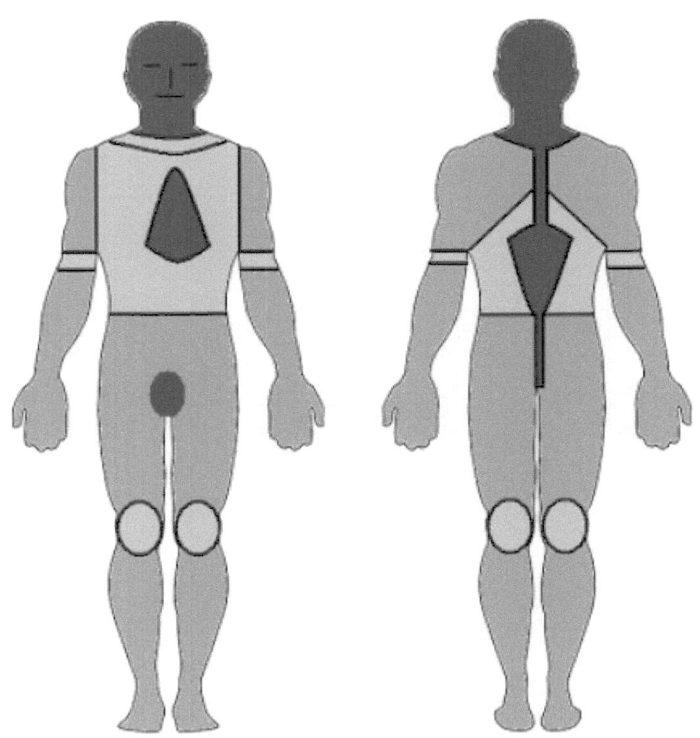

When using stunning techniques an Warrior must be mindful that there is no safe area on the body which to target. The effects of any stunning technique on a subjects body is nearly impossible to predict. The study of conflict anatomy can give the Warrior only probable answers at best. An Warrior must take into account the totality of circumstances when using stunning techniques. The amount of force necessary to be effective or in the inverse, use excessive force will depend on many factors. Size is one easily identifiable factor. A smaller, physically less powerful Warrior may not expect the same effect of a stun that a large powerful Warrior might. The size of the subject must also be taken into consideration when evaluating which stunning techniques are most appropriate. The stunning targets and their effects presented here are a general guideline used for informative and illustrative purposes only. Ultimately an Warrior must abide by their agency's use of force policy, as well as any local state and federal laws which pertain to use of force before using physical force on a subject in either capacity as an Warrior or civilian.

Presented below are targets for stunning targets divided into three levels.

LEVEL I TARGETS

Level one represents targets on a subject's body which when affected are unlikely to cause serious or permanent injury to a subject. These targets should be viewed as a primary option. Level Two represents targets on a subject's body which when effected are likely to cause a higher level of temporary and/or permanent trauma than Level One Targets.

Forearm	**Buttocks**	**Back of Hand**
Shoulder	**Lower abdomen**	**Inside of wrist**
Shoulder Blades	**Upper Arm**	**Shin**
Calf	**Achilles tendon**	**Thigh**
Instep		

LEVEL II TARGETS

A stun to a level two target has a higher risk for significant injury to a subject. A transition from a level one to a level two target should be considered by the Warrior when

(1)A Level One target proves ineffective in controlling the subject.

(2) A Level One target is inaccessible. (3)When a subject must be immediately controlled.

Knee Joint	**Elbow Joint**
Rib Cage	**Collar Bone**

LEVEL III TARGETS

Level Three targets are last resort lethal force targets. An office should never attempt a stun to these targets unless the Warrior fears that the subject posses a threat of death or seriously injure to the Warrior or another.

Spine	Ear	Bridge of Nose	Eyes
Kidney	Throat	Lower Jaw	Tail Bone
Solar Plexus	Neck	Temple	Upper Jaw
Base of Neck	Groin		

TYPES OF STRIKES

In employing the baton, Warriors will use two primary types of strikes. The two are explained below.

1. FOLLOW THROUGH STRIKE

For this type of strike the Warrior should swing the baton at the desired target with the intention of completing the arc of the swing. This is the more powerful of the two types of strikes. The Follow through strike however has a slower recovery time than the Retracting Strike.

2. RETRACTING STRIKE

For this type of strike the Warrior should swing the baton at the desired target. Once impact has been made the Warrior will rapidly retract the baton. This is the less powerful of the two types of strikes. The Retracting Strike however has a much faster recovery time than the Follow through Strike.

ANGLES OF ATTACK

Striking techniques, thrusts or swings will be executed on particular lines of attack. All other attacks will come on one of the lines illustrated below. There are 11 angles of attack, of which 8 are the primary work horse angles used for common defense. For this reason the majority of the striking techniques shown in this book are only used demonstrating the essential 8 angles. The reader however should know that there are an additional 3 angles that can be used.

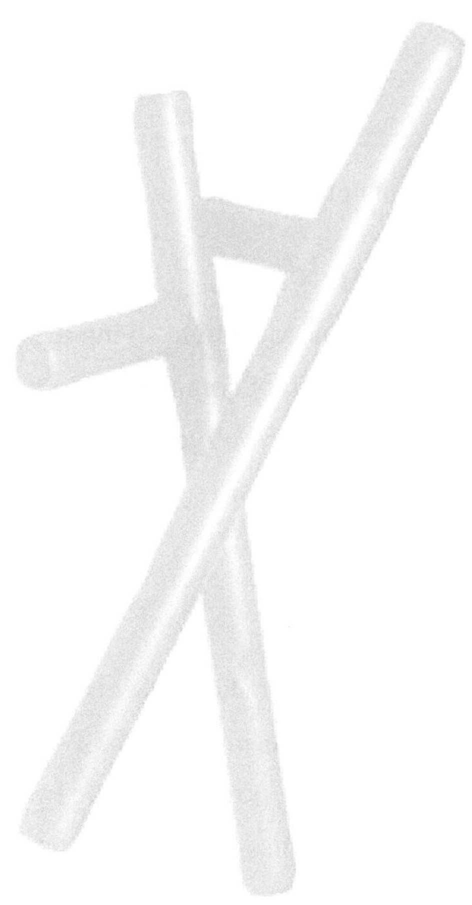

ESSENTIAL EIGHT STRIKING ANGLES

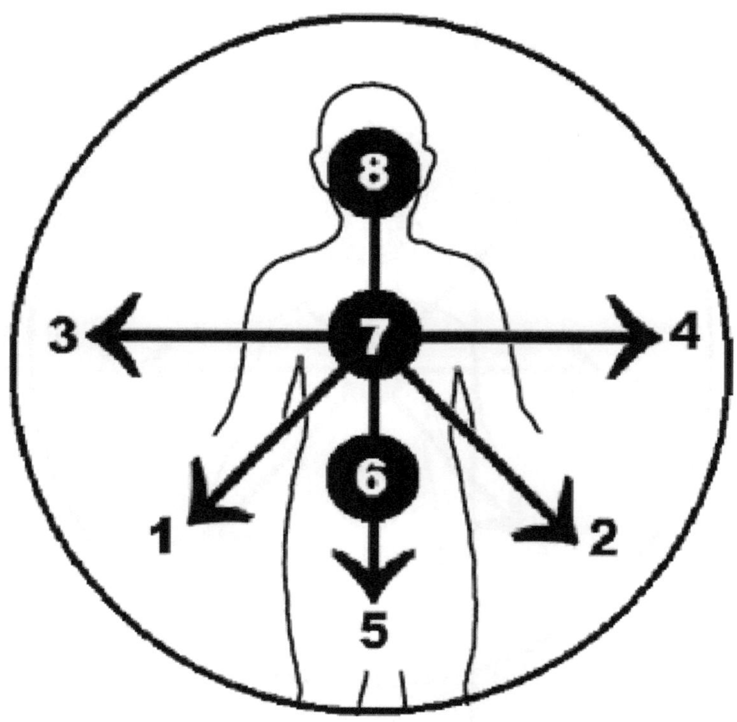

Angle One: A downward diagonal swing

Angle 1: Forehand downward diagonal

Angle 2: Backhand downward diagonal

Angle 3: A horizontal swing to the Inside

Angle 4: A horizontal swing to the out side

Angle 5: Forehand Upward diagonal

Angle 6-8: A jabbing, lunging, or punching attack directed straight toward the warrior's front. It can be delivered from any height.

COMPLETE 11 STRIKING ANGLES

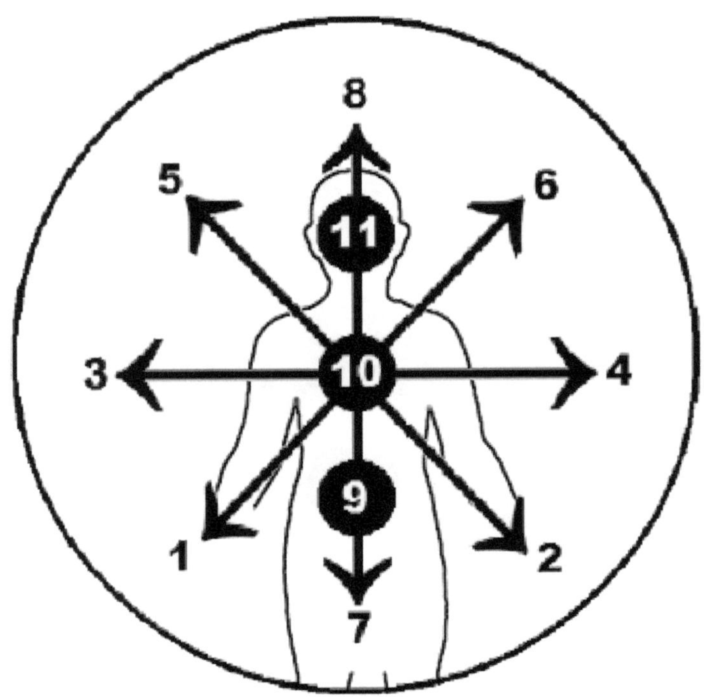

Angle One: A downward diagonal swing

Angle 1: Forehand downward diagonal

Angle 2: Backhand downward diagonal

Angle 3: A horizontal swing to the Inside

Angle 4: A horizontal swing to the out side

Angle 5: Forehand Upward diagonal

Angle 6: Backhand Upward diagonal

Angle 7: Upward vertical

Angel 8 Downward Diagonal

Angle 9-11: A jabbing, lunging, or punching attack directed straight toward the warrior's front. It can be delivered from any height.

STRIKING TECHNIQUES

EXTENDED TONFA GRIP: FOREHAND DIAGONAL CHOP

To execute the forehand diagonal chop the warrior will raise the baton to shoulder level and then swing downward on the diagonal line. The warrior will make contact with the entire underside of the baton shaft as the striking surface.

EXTENDED TONFA GRIP: BACK HAND DIAGONAL CHOP

To execute the back hand diagonal chop the warrior will raise the baton to shoulder level and then swing downward on the diagonal line. The warrior will make contact with the entire underside of the baton shaft as the striking surface.

EXTENDED TONFA GRIP: HORIZONTAL FOREHAND STRIKE

To execute the forehand horizontal strike the warrior will hold the baton to their side and then swing horizontally across the body. The warrior will make contact with the last four inches of the baton shaft as the striking surface.

EXTENDED TONFA GRIP: HORIZONTAL BACKHAND STRIKE

To execute the backhand horizontal strike the warrior will hold the baton to their inside and then swing horizontally across the body. The warrior will make contact with the last four inches of the baton shaft as the striking surface.

EXTENDED TONFA GRIP: VERTICAL CHOP

To execute the vertical chop the warrior will raise the baton to shoulder level and then swing downward on the vertical line. The warrior will make contact with the entire underside of the baton shaft as the striking surface. The attack can also be executed from low to high in a rising manner.

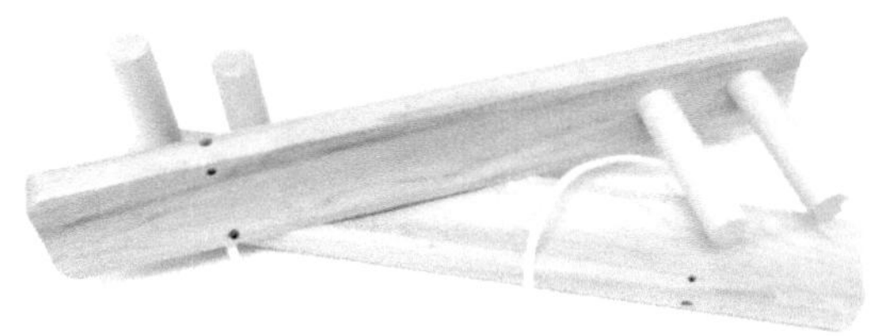

REVERSE GRIP: DIAGONAL FOREHAND STRIKE

To execute the forehand diagonal strike the warrior will raise the baton to shoulder level and then swing downward on the diagonal line. The warrior will make contact with the last four inches of the baton shaft as the striking surface.

REVERSE GRIP: DIAGONAL BACKHAND STRIKE

To execute the back hand diagonal strike the warrior will raise the baton to shoulder level and then swing downward on the diagonal line. The warrior will make contact with the last four inches of the baton shaft as the striking surface.

REVERSE GRIP: HORIZONTAL FOREHAND STRIKE

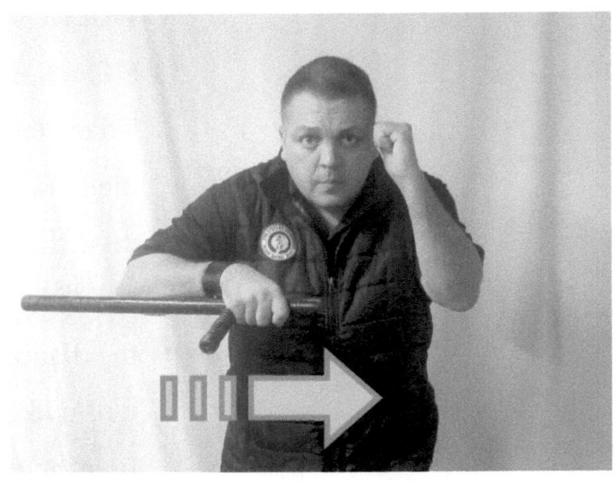

To execute the forehand horizontal strike the warrior will hold the baton to their side and then swing horizontally across the body. The warrior will make contact with the last four inches of the baton shaft as the striking surface.

REVERSE GRIP: HORIZONTAL BACKHAND STRIKE

To execute the backhand horizontal strike the warrior will hold the baton to their inside and then swing horizontally across the body. The warrior will make contact with the last four inches of the baton shaft as the striking surface.

REVERSE GRIP: VERTICAL STRIKE

To execute the vertical strike the warrior will raise the baton to shoulder level and then swing downward on the vertical line. The warrior will make contact with the last four inches of the baton shaft as the striking surface. The strike can also be executed from low to high in a rising manner.

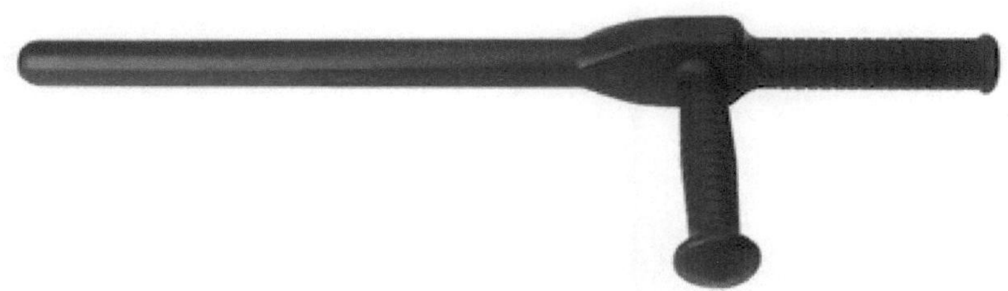

BATON GRIP: DIAGONAL FOREHAND STRIKE

To execute the forehand diagonal strike the warrior will raise the baton to shoulder level and then swing downward on the diagonal line. The warrior will make contact with the last four inches of the baton shaft as the striking surface.

BATON GRIP: DIAGONAL BACKHAND STRIKE

To execute the back hand diagonal strike the warrior will raise the baton to shoulder level and then swing downward on the diagonal line. The warrior will make contact with the last four inches of the baton shaft as the striking surface.

BATON GRIP: HORIZONTAL FOREHAND STRIKE

To execute the forehand horizontal strike the warrior will hold the baton to their side and then swing horizontally across the body. The warrior will make contact with the last four inches of the baton shaft as the striking surface.

BATON GRIP: HORIZONTAL BACKHAND STRIKE

To execute the backhand horizontal strike the warrior will hold the baton to their inside and then swing horizontally across the body. The warrior will make contact with the last four inches of the baton shaft as the striking surface.

BATON GRIP: DOWNWARD VERTICAL STRIKE

To execute the vertical strike the warrior will raise the baton to shoulder level and then swing downward on the vertical line. The warrior will make contact with the last four inches of the baton shaft as the striking surface.

OBSTRUCTED ATTACK SOLUTIONS

OBSTRUCTED ATTACK SOLUTIONS

There will be times when the Warrior is attempting to complete and attack and the subject creates an obstruction to this attack. The Warrior has several ways to properly address the obstructed attack. They include:

-Pulling the obstructing limb
-Pushing the obstructed limb
-Taking a secondary line of attack

OBSTRUCTED ATTACK SOLUTION: THE PULL

1. The assailant blocks and obstructs the Warrior's initial attack.
2. The Warrior uses his free hand to pull the obstruction away
3. The Warrior is then free to counter attack if needed.

OBSTRUCTED ATTACK SOLUTION: THE PUSH

1. The assailant blocks and obstructs the Warrior's initial attack.
2. The Warrior uses his free hand to push the obstruction away
3. The Warrior is then free to counter attack if needed.

OBSTRUCTED ATTACK SOLUTION: SECONDARY LINES

1. The assailant blocks and obstructs the Warrior's initial attack.
2. The Warrior pulls his initial attack away from the obstruction and finds an unobstructed path on which to complete the attack.
3. The Warrior is then free to counter attack if needed.

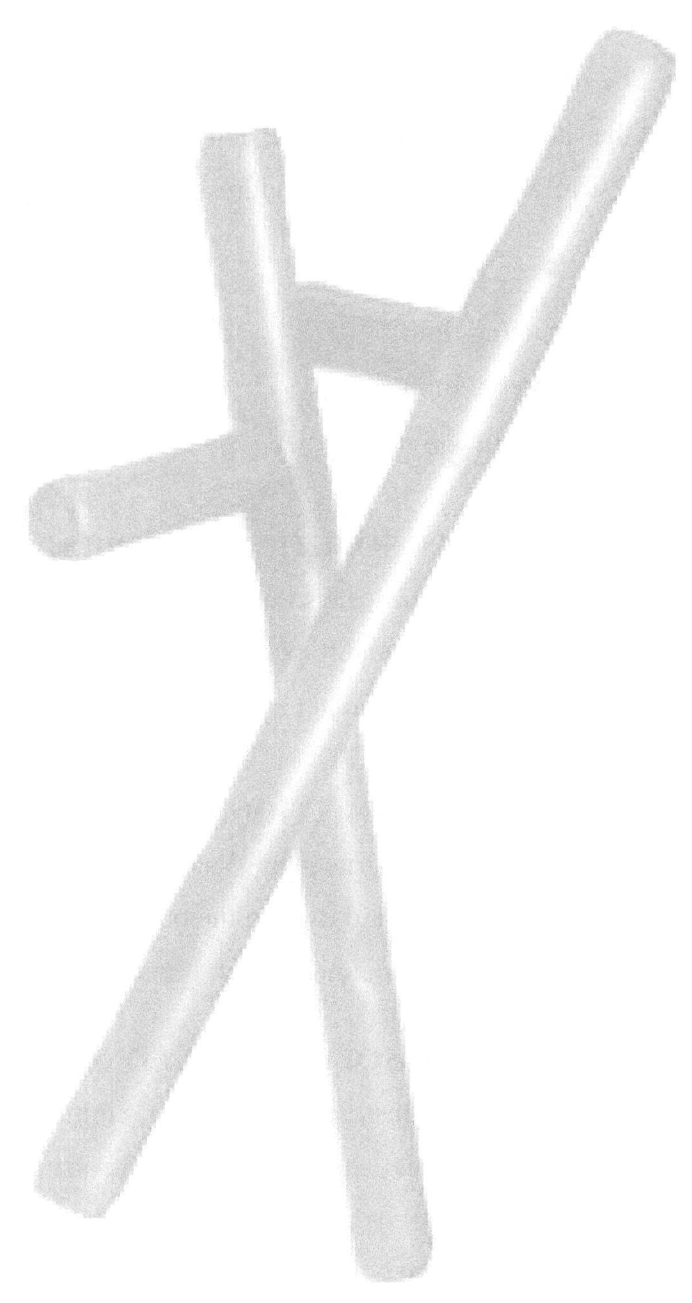

DRILLS & EXERCISES

FUNCTIONAL DRILLS

Our System uses a variety of simple drills to enhance the Warrior's ability to successfully deal with a weapon assault. The drills are designed to emphasize specific components which give the Warrior ample time to develop the appropriate attributes needed to use the skills successfully. While most of the drills in the system are easy to learn and use, regular practice is still recommended. It is also recommended that each component be practiced as individual skill-sets before putting them together to create a complete response.

DEFLECT & DISENGAGE DRILL

For this drill two partners will pair up. One will be the attacker and the other will be the warrior. The partners will begin by standing 7-21 feet from each other. The attacker will then feed the warrior an attack. The warrior will attempt to move off line and avoid the attack, using their baton to deflect and redirect the incoming attack. Once the attack is deflected the warrior should attempt to disengage and get out of measure. The attacker will continue to attack the warrior from various angles. The attacks can be predetermined and then gradually become random. The speed and intensity of the attacks can also be gradually increased.

DEFLECT & ENGAGE DRILL

For this drill two partners will pair up. One will be the attacker and the other will be the warrior. The partners will begin by standing 7 feet or less from each other. Where the goal in the previous drill was to avoid and separate from the attacker, the goal of this drill is to avoid the initial attack and close the distance to counter attack. The attacker will continue to attack the warrior from various angles. The attacks can be predetermined and then gradually become random. The speed and intensity of the attacks can also be gradually increased.

SPONTANEOUS DEFENSE DRILL

To perform this drill, multiple subjects will surround and circle the Warrior. The subjects will take turns randomly attacking the Warrior. The attacks will be staggered so the Warrior can not time the attacks. The Warrior should defend and counter attack this drill will assist the Warrior in inoculating themselves to ambush or surprise attacks.

MEET & FOLLOW THE FORCE

One excellent drill for developing hand-eye coordination, timing and reaction time is the Meet & Follow Force Drill. As the assailant Attacks the Warrior, the Warrior will meet the incoming attack with his weapon, coming to the inside of the opponent's arc of power. Meeting the force is most often a proactive way of addressing an incoming attack.

FOLLOW THE FORCE DRILL SERIES

As the assailant Attacks the Warrior , the Warrior is not prepared and is not quick enough to meet the incoming attack with his weapon, coming to the inside of the opponents arc of power. The Warrior then uses body movement to avoid the attack and then address the attack on the "back end" by following the attack. Following the force is a most often a Reactive way of addressing an incoming attack.

MEET THE FORCE/FOLLOW THE FORCE ADD ONS

Once the Warrior has mastered these two basic drills the Warrior can build upon them in the following ways. Once the Warrior addresses the initial attack the Warrior will adjust their position and then execute one of the following.

DOWNWARD DIAGONAL ATTACKS

Once the Warrior has addressed the initial attack, the Warrior will execute forehand downward diagonal attack followed by a back hand downward diagonal attack.

UPWARD DIAGONAL ATTACKS

Once the Warrior has addressed the initial attack, the Warrior will execute forehand upward diagonal attack followed by a back hand upward diagonal attack.

HORIZONTAL ATTACKS

Once the Warrior has addressed the initial attack, the Warrior will execute forehand horizontal attack followed by a back hand horizontal attack.

THRUSTING ATTACKS

Once the Warrior has addressed the initial attack, the Warrior will execute two thrusting attacks.

HIT AND GRAB DRILL

In this drill the Warrior will practice bringing the live hand into play. The goal of the drill is to develop the Warrior's ability to defend with the baton and immediately use the live hand to seize the enemy's arm either at the wrist or the forearm. This drill can be performed in a few different ways. To begin the Enemy will feed the Warrior the series of angles from any of the established patterns or templates. The enemy can also opt to feed angles randomly. The Warrior in response will either meet the enemy's force or follow it, defending with the baton by either hitting the enemy's arm or using a block. Once the Warrior has successfully defended the initial attack they will then reach in with the live hand and seize the enemy's arm at the forearm or wrist. The Warrior can make the seizure from either the inside or the outside of the enemy's arm. The better the grip of the Warrior the more effective the skill will be in combat.

SPONTANEOUS DEFENSE DRILL

To perform this drill, multiple subjects will surround and circle the Warrior. The subjects will take turns randomly attacking the Warrior. The attacks will be staggered so the Warrior can not time the attacks. The Warrior should use techniques and concepts taught in the course to address the attacks. This drill will assist the Warrior in inoculating themselves to ambush or surprise attacks.

3-2-1 DRILL

In this drill, one partner will attack and freeze for 3 seconds. In those three seconds the other partner should counter and attack in a spontaneous fashion. At the end of the three seconds the attacking partner will then break away and attack again. The purpose of this drill is to allow the Warrior to acquire target acquisition skills, proper coordination, attack sequencing and timing. Once the Warrior feels comfortable with 3 seconds, the drill should drop down to 2 seconds and finally one second. This progression will lead the Warrior to real time sparring and scenarios by gradually building the skill level needed for a more realistic tempo in training.

IMPAIRMENT DRILLS

In the chaos of combat there is no guarantee of ideal conditions. If an Warrior has never faced combat or contest under stress or duress they may find themselves in for a rude awakening. While I do not advocate that an Warrior go out and seek the lessons of true combat I do advocate the simulation of conditions they may find in such. There are several simple things that the Warrior can do to simulate these conditions. The more the Warrior is exposed to these impairments the better prepared they will be to fight through them. Just as a block or evasion is trained as a proper response to an attack, the Warrior will train their bodies to respond correctly when faced with injury or stress.

STROBE LIGHT DRILL

One of the best drills I ever learned was given to me by Grand Master Gus Michalik. G.M. Gus shared with me the wonders of strobe light training and sparring. A strobe light gives the visual illusion of slow motion, something often reported as an effect of high stress encounters. A strobe light can also be very disorienting. Both of these conditions are perfect for taking an Warrior out of their comfort zone. Warriors who train under the strobe light will be able to experience a very chaotic environment which in many ways mimics the realities of combat stress. By training under these conditions the Warrior can become familiar with the feeling of disorientation and therefore learn to perform in less than ideal conditions. For this drill I recommend an industrial strobe light. I have rented them from lighting companies in the past for about $50.00 a day. The small ones you can buy at the novelty store usually won't be able to give you the effect you need, as they don't flash as powerfully or frequently.

APACHE VISIBILITY TRAINING

My friend and Apache Battle Tactics instructor Snake Blocker has a panache for training drills. He is one of the best sources I have found for interesting training drills. Snake has made a career of collecting and cataloging traditional Apache games and drills which relate directly to combat training. Here are a few of my favorite drills which Snake has shared with me. Taking a page out of the Apache play book, Warriors can practice all of their drills, training sets and sparring in a variety of lighting conditions. The goal is to accustom the Warrior to the various lighting conditions which they may encounter. The three conditions under which the Warrior should train are:

STAGE ONE: DAY LIGHT/FULL LIGHT: PHOTOPIC VISION

Photopic visual conditions allow for high visual acuity and color perception. Under these conditions light is processed by the cones of the eyes.

STAGE TWO: MID LIGHT: MESOPIC VISION

Mesopic vision is used in low light conditions which are not totally dark. In the mesopic range the eyes use both the cones and rods to process light. A common example of mesopic conditions would be a city street at night lit by street lights and other ambient light. These lighting conditions are very common to a variety of assault scenarios. It is crucial for an Warrior to practice their art under these conditions. While it is very possible to be robbed or assaulted in the light of day, many criminals will choose to mask their acts at night.

STAGE THREE: LOW LIGHT/NO LIGHT: SCOTOPIC VISION

Under scotopic visual conditions the eyes process light exclusively with the rods. Scotopic visual conditions will range from very low light to no light at all. Color discrimination is virtually non-existent under these conditions and visual acuity is very low. Warriors will find these conditions to be the most challenging in training. Because vision is so impaired under these conditions extra attention to safety in training must be a consideration.

THE CIRCLE OF DEATH

To perform this drill, multiple assailants will surround and circle the Warrior. The assailants will take turns randomly attacking the Warrior. The attacks will be staggered so the Warrior can not time the attacks. This drill will assist the Warrior in inoculating themselves to ambush or surprise attacks.

BLURRY VISION

If the Warrior is using eye wear (as they always should) a swipe of lip balm across the lenses of their goggles can be used to impair vision. Also see the section on Drills and visual concepts in this book for further ideas on how to train the vision for all combat conditions.

DIZZINESS

Remember when you were 5 yrs old and would spin around until you were dizzy? Try the same trick before a sparring session. The dizziness can mimic the impaired equilibrium you may face if you took a good shot to the head or were loosing blood from a wound.

LOSS OF LIMB

A gnarled and damaged limb can definitely put a cramp in your style. Have you trained for it? If not you should start now. It is as easy as putting one hand in your pocket or behind your back. Switch to your off hand or splint your leg to simulate a damaged one. As mentioned in previous chapters a little oil on the hand can train the Warrior to hold onto a baton with a blood soaked hand. All of these simple tricks can help the Warrior learn how to adapt to an injured body.

SPARRING

In my humble opinion no drill is more useful and yet more incorrectly used than sparring. Yes, sparring is a drill. It is not a match. The difference is very clear. In a match both parties are intent on besting the other, the purpose is a test of skill. In a sparring drill the purpose is training a skill, not testing it. If you are sparring without a specific goal, and without pre and post sparring instruction, then you are not sparring. You are having a match. While many take this approach in training I feel it is a mistake. A student could match 1000 times a day and still never see improvement absent instruction. Presented here are a few of my favorite sparring variations. I encourage all readers to expand and modify the variations presented. I also encourage the reader to innovate their own variations. Remember, sparring is a goal oriented drill. All sparring should have clear parameters and goals. These should be monitored closely by the instructor or senior practitioner present.

ISOLATION SPARRING

In "isolation sparring" the Warrior will focus on one particular technique or tactic. An Warrior may for example dedicate their sparring session to the working of thrusting techniques. The sparring partner will be free to feed any techniques they like but the Warrior will focus on answering those attacks with thrusting techniques. Attacks, foot work, defenses, all can be used in a variety of isolation sparring sessions to advance the Warriors skill.

IMPAIRMENT SPARRING

In the chaos of combat there is no guarantee of ideal conditions. If an Warrior has never faced combat or contest under stress or duress they may find themselves in for a rude awakening. While I do not advocate that an Warrior go out and seek the lessons of true combat I do advocate the simulation of conditions they may find in such. There are several simple things that the Warrior can do to simulate these conditions. The more the Warrior is exposed to these impairments the better prepared they will be to fight through them. Just as a block or evasion is trained as a proper response to an attack, the Warrior will train their bodies to respond correctly when faced with injury or stress.

VISUAL

If the Warrior is using eye wear (as they always should) a swipe of lip balm across the lenses of their goggles can be used to impair vision. Also see the section on Drills and visual concepts in this book for further ideas on how to train the vision for all combat conditions.

DIZZINESS

Remember when you were 5 yrs old and would spin around until you were dizzy? Try the same trick before a sparring session. The dizziness can mimic the impaired equilibrium you may face if you took a good shot to the head or were loosing blood from a wound.

LOSS OF LIMB

A gnarled and damaged limb can definitely put a cramp in your style. Have you trained for it? If not you should start now. It is as easy as putting one hand in your pocket or behind your back. Switch to your off hand or splint your leg to simulate a damaged one. As mentioned in previous chapters a little oil on the hand can train the Warrior to hold onto a baton with a blood soaked hand. All of these simple tricks can help the Warrior learn how to adapt to an injured body.

COMBAT STRESS

Muscles tighten, breath is labored, and your focus is challenged. These are just a few of the things that you can expect to experience under the stressful conditions of combat. When the fight or flight response is triggered the body draws blood from the extremities to the core and vital organs. Do you know what else triggers these changes? COLD. A little sparring out doors in the winter or a bucket of ice cold water in the summer is all that you need to experience these feelings.

PHONE BOOTH SPARRING

While I love the long range game, and would choose it 9 out of 10 times if given the option, we must train for the extreme close quarter engagement as well. What if you're assaulted between parked cars in a parking lot, in a tight corridor or in an elevator? To train this range, use tape on the floor to create a small box and spar inside of it. Doing so will force you to work different skills such as your checking hands, trapping and more.

MIXED WEAPONS SPARRING

Baton VS empty hand is one thing but baton VS chain, baseball bat, or folding chair is another. The Warrior should take time to partake in mixed weapon sparring sessions. Doing so will prepare the Warrior for the differences in reach, speed, and many other variable presented by different weapons.

TOTAL BODY SPARRING

Total body sparring will see the Warrior engage in sparring that involves not only their baton but their other weapons as well, hands feet, elbows, etc. In this sparring drill the Warrior will learn to incorporate strikes and blows as well as the attacks of their baton.

BATON CHOKES

CHOKE HOLDS: REAR CROSS CHOKE

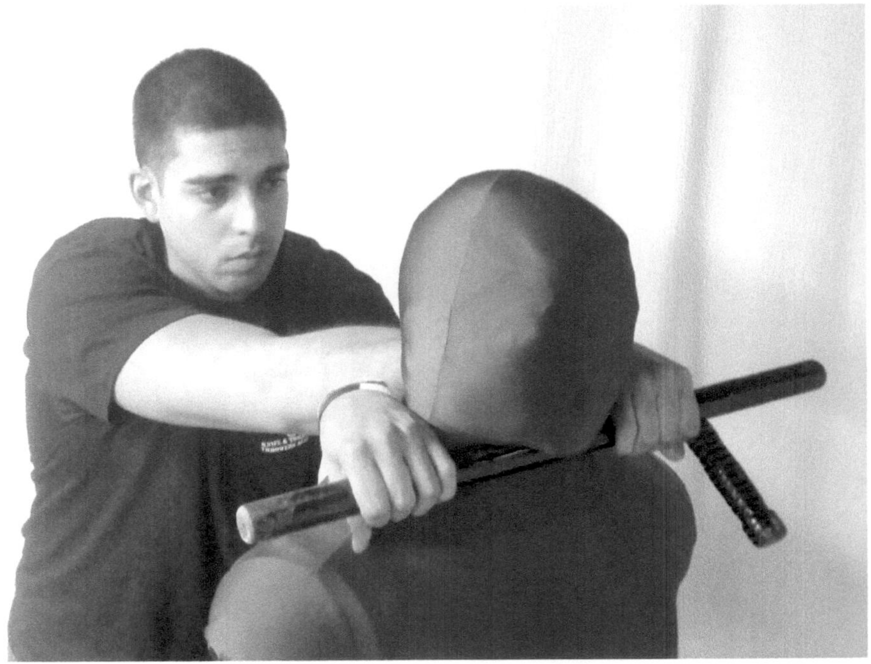

The technique is applied by holding the baton in a reverse grip. The Warrior should place their wrist on the subject's neck on the same side. This will place the shaft of the baton across the subject's throat. The Warrior should then cross his free hand and grip the baton shaft on the other side. The Warrior should have both wrists close to the subject's neck. Once secured the Warrior squeeze tight and pull his hands to his navel. **This is a lethal force technique.*

CHOKE HOLDS: REAR CHOKE

To execute the rear choke, the Warrior must start by placing the baton across the subject's neck or throat. Once the baton is in place the Warrior will insert their free hand and place the end shaft of the baton in the pit of the elbow of the free hand. The Warrior next will place his free hand behind the subjects head at the base of the skull. The Warrior now will simultaneously push the head down, while squeezing his elbows in tight to his own body and extending his lateral muscles. **This is a lethal force technique.*

CHOKE HOLDS: REAR PULLING CHOKE

To execute the rear pulling choke, the Warrior must first extend the baton across the subject's neck directly below their chin. The Warrior's hands should be snug on both sides of the subject's neck. The Warrior then secures the baton from both sides and pulls both hands to his own waist while stepping back to ensure the subject does not fall directly on him. **This is a lethal force technique.*

CHOKE HOLDS: FRONT CROSS CHOKE

The technique is applied by holding the baton in a reverse grip. The Warrior should place their wrist on the subject's neck on the same side. This will place the shaft of the baton across the back of the subject's neck. The Warrior should then cross his free hand and grip the baton shaft on the other side. The Warrior should have both wrists close to the subject's neck. Once secured the Warrior squeeze tight and pull his hands to his navel. **This is a lethal force technique.*

CHOKE HOLDS: DIAGONAL PULLING CHOKE

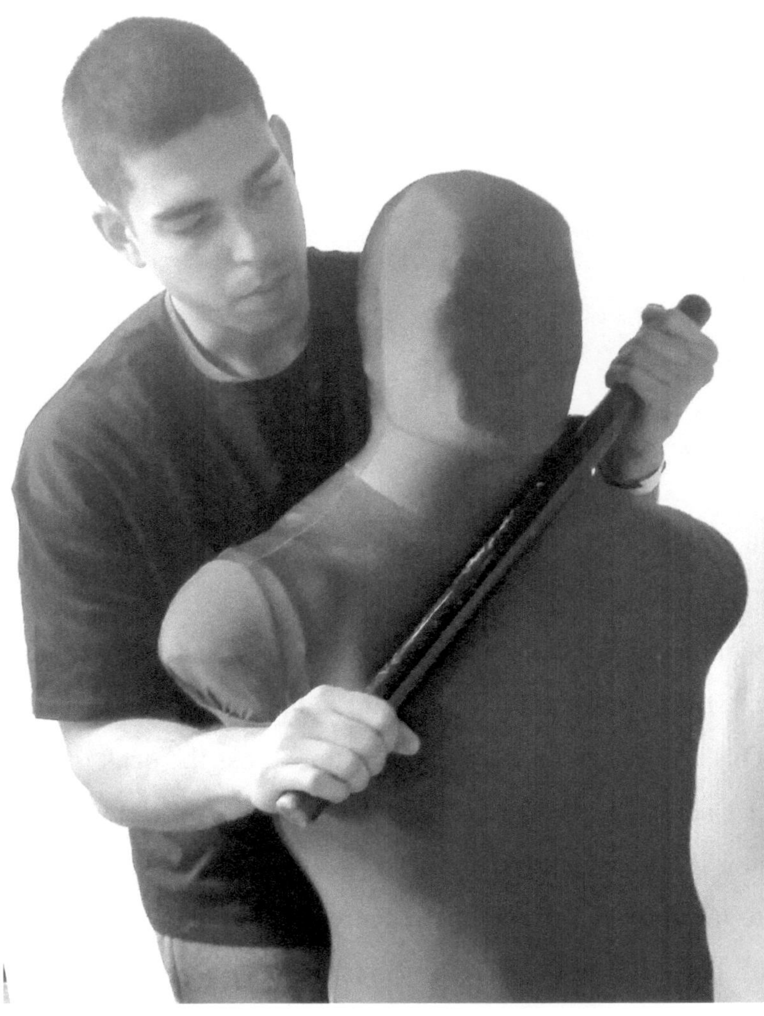

To execute the rear Diagonal pulling choke, the Warrior must first extend the baton under the subjects arm pit and across the chest. The Warrior will grip the baton on the opposite end. The Warrior then secures the baton from both sides and pulls both hands to his own waist while stepping back to ensure the subject does not fall directly on him. **This is a lethal force technique.*

CHOKE HOLDS: BODY CHOKE

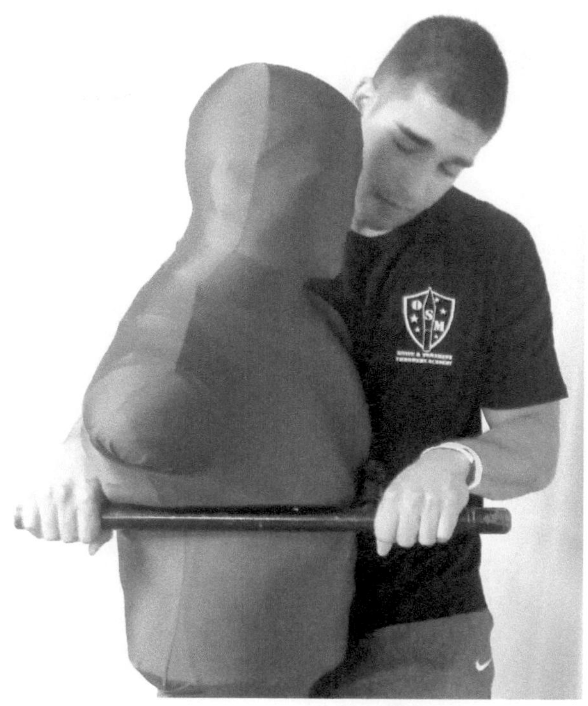

Begin by wrapping the baton around the assailants ribs. Next, simultaneously pull the baton towards your own torso and pushing into the assailant with your shoulder. Make sure your head is to the outside of the assailant's body. When pulling, pull in on a slightly upward angle. This technique will create intense pain. The technique will also make it difficult for the assailant to breath. Note that there is a serious risk of breaking ribs and creating internal damage. This technique must be considered only when lethal force is the only option. .

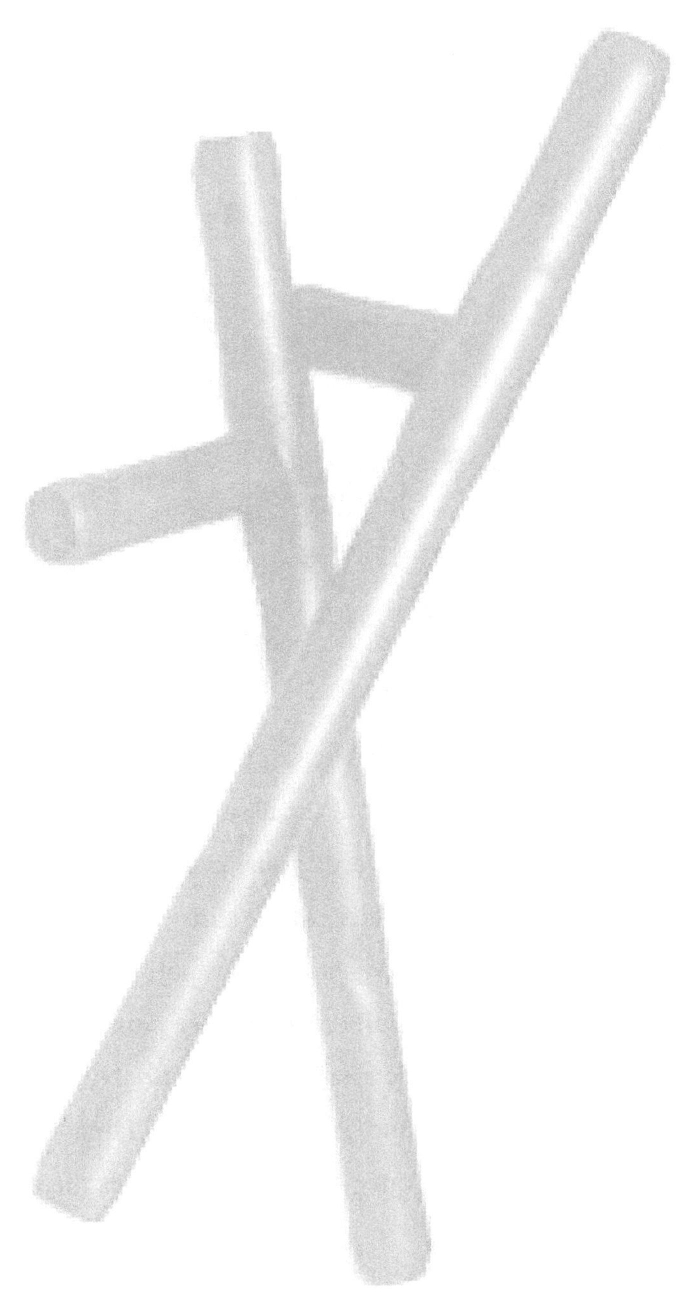

BATON TAKE DOWNS

TAKE DOWN: HIP PULL TAKE DOWN

Begin by wrapping the baton around the assailants back. Lower the baton around the assailant's waist while simultaneously pulling the baton towards your own torso and pushing into the assailant with your shoulder. Make sure your head is to the outside of the assailant's body. Once the assailant begins to loose balance, release one side of the baton to release the assailant so they fall to the ground without the Warrior going to the ground. A safer variation of the take down which does not go against the spine is pictured in the second photograph. Here the Warrior wraps behind the subjects buttocks rather than the swell of the back. the take down is equally effective.

DOUBLE LEG TAKEDOWN

Begin by wrapping the baton around the assailants back. Lower the baton around the assailant's waist while simultaneously pulling the baton towards your own torso and pushing into the assailant with your shoulder. Make sure your head is to the outside of the assailant's body. Once the assailant begins to loose balance, Drop the baton behind their knees and continue to drive with the shoulder. Release one side of the baton to release the assailant so they fall to the ground without the Warrior going to the ground.

HEAD PULL TAKE DOWN

To execute the head pull take down, the Warrior must first extend the baton across back of the subject's neck. The Warrior's hands should be snug on both sides of the subject's neck. The Warrior then secures the baton from both sides and pulls both hands to his own waist while stepping back to ensure the subject does not fall directly on him.

GROIN PULL/LEG PULL TAKE DOWN

To execute the pulling takedown the Warrior will grab the enemy across the chest and simultaneously place their hawk under the enemy's groin or the back of their leg. The Warrior will then push with their live hand and pull with their hawk hand while driving forward causing the enemy to fall backwards.

ARM DRAG TAKE DOWN

To execute the arm drag take down the Warrior will begin by grabbing the enemy's wrist. The Warrior will then place their hawk against the enemy's forearm. Once the hawk is resting on the enemy's forearm the Warrior will apply pressure downwards as they simultaneously pivot and pull with their live hand to bring the enemy down.

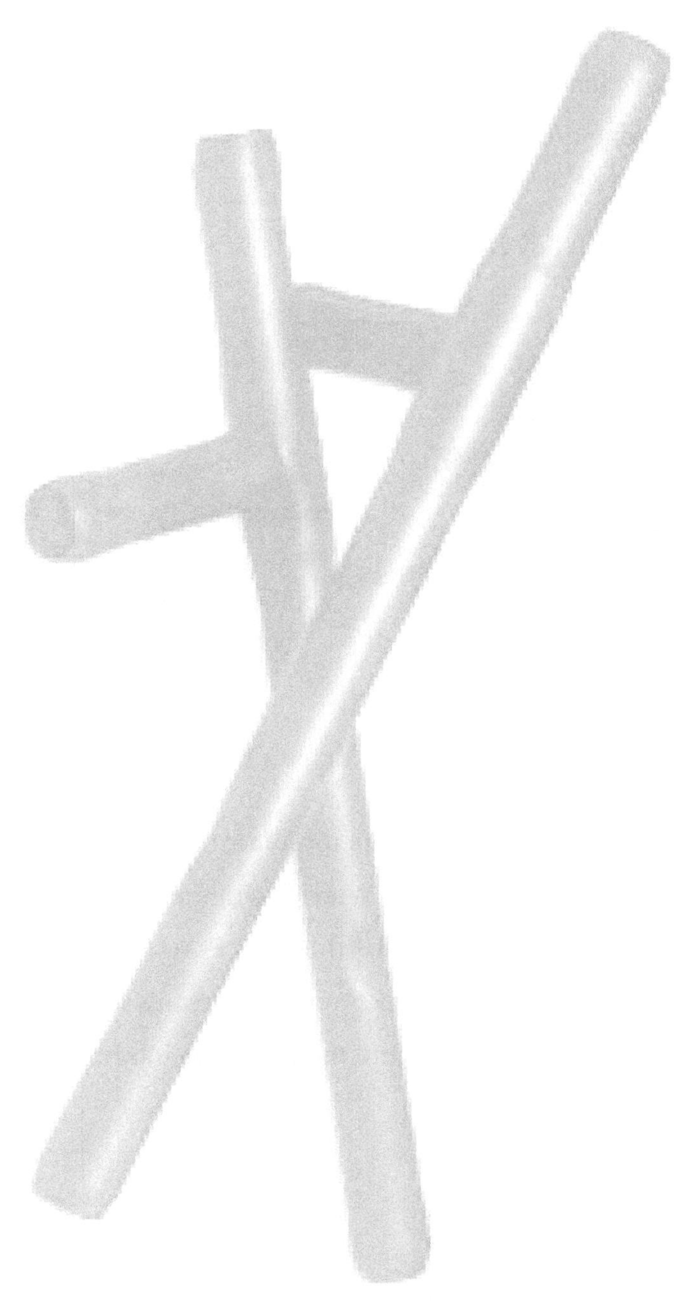

GROUND TECHNIQUES

GROUND APPLICATIONS

There are times when an Warrior may find themselves on the ground during an altercation. If the Warrior finds themselves in this position they should first seek to establish a good defensive position and then Safely make the transition back to the standing position. Warrior's should practice applying all of the standing baton techniques on the on the ground as well, as they translate effectively. Some considerations must be made as well as adjustments but the overall theories and strategies are still very sound. Bellow is a series of sequences which are meant to be a small skill set. The Warrior must add to this skill set through the use flexible application of the standing core techniques to ground situations. This will be best accomplished by the use of Functional training drill.

Warriors should also note that Ground techniques are potentially lethal force scenarios for two reasons. 1. The Warrior is in a compromised position where they are not able to properly defend themselves and 2. because in order to apply some of the ground fighting techniques the Warrior must apply stress to the joints, and other areas such as the spine, or kidneys. Even though the Warrior is applying slow direct pressure and not impact force, the effected areas of the subject's body are sensitive and the Warrior can not ensure that the application of the technique will be 100% safe for the subject.

MOUNT DEFENSE #1

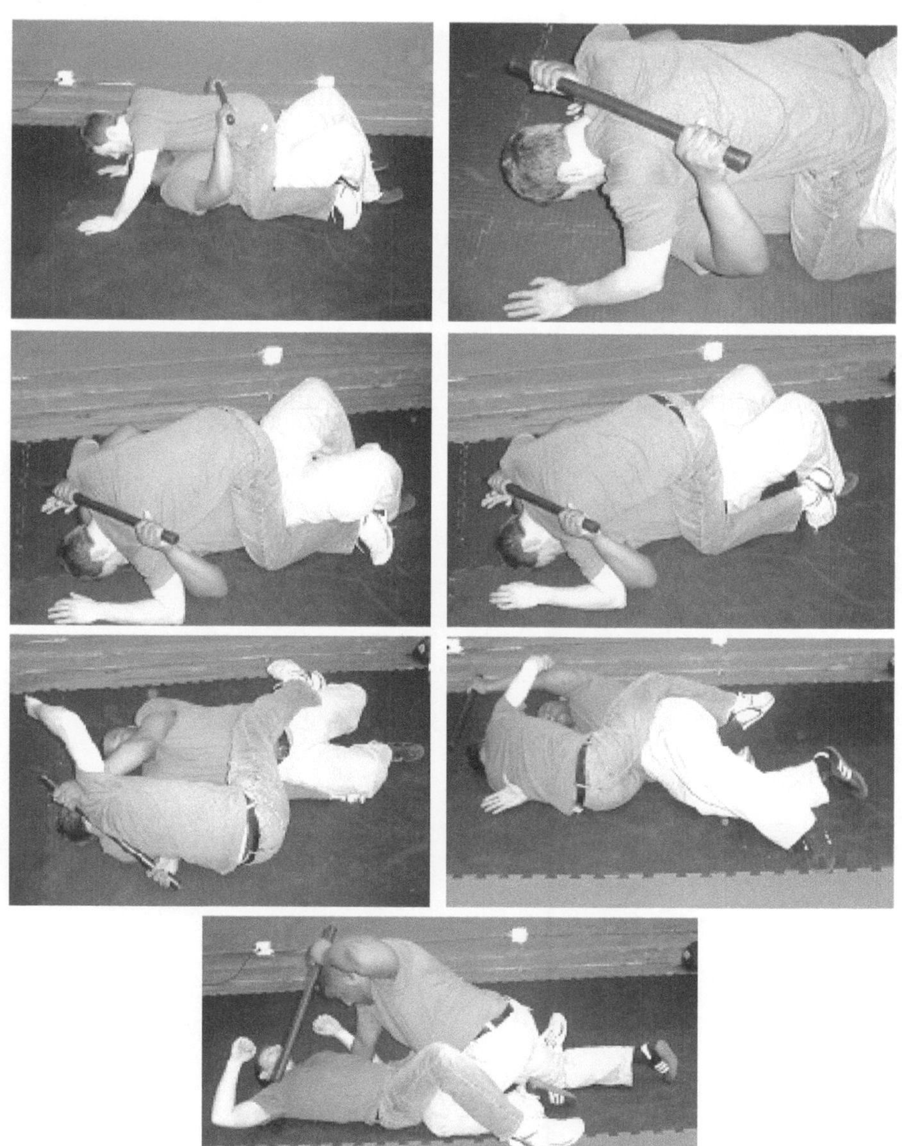

The Warrior finds himself mounted by the subject. The Warrior wraps the baton around the subjects back. The Warrior brings the baton across the subjects shoulder. The Warrior pulls the subject into him towards the ground.

The Warrior now raises his hips, further putting the subject off balance. The Warrior now rolls to towards the subject's trapped shoulder, rolling the subject off of the Warrior. The Warrior then assumes a ready position, where he can strike or disengage.

SCISSOR SWEEP

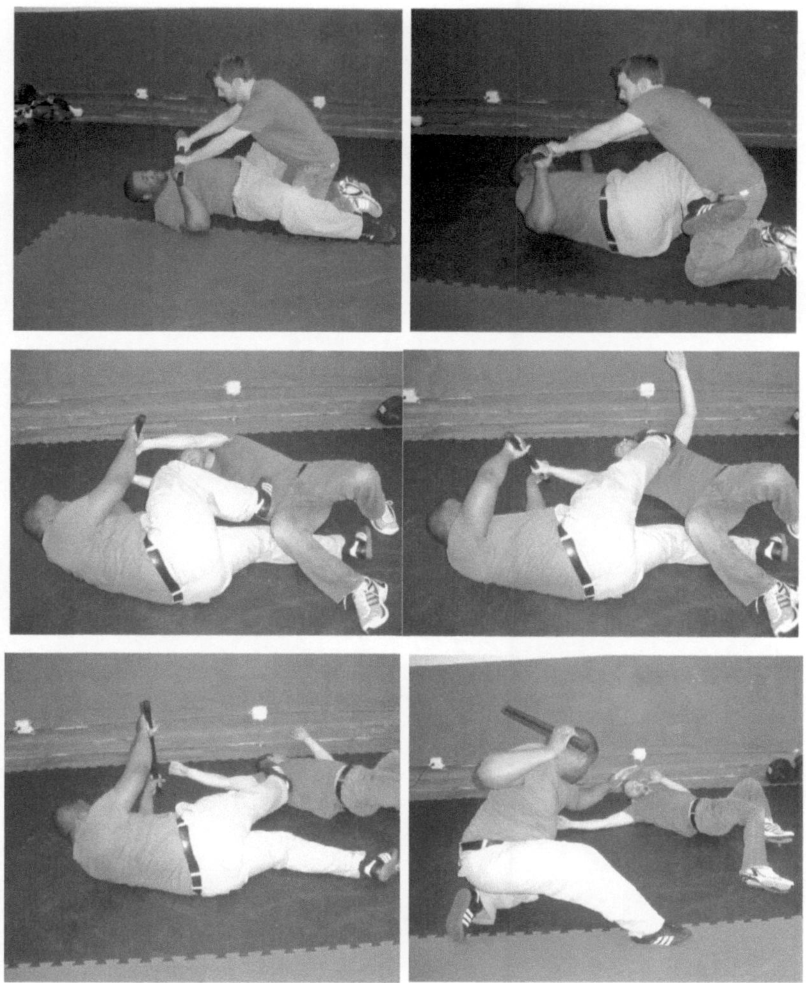

The Warrior finds the subject in his guard fighting for the Warrior's baton. The subject has two hands on the baton. Turn to side, and then Scissor your legs, while pulling the secured arm. Once the subject has been taken over, the Warrior kicks the subjects arm to free his grip on the baton. The Warrior then kicks to the other arm to free the baton entirely. The Warrior now assumes a defensive stance while returning to his feet.

MOUNT DEFENSE #2

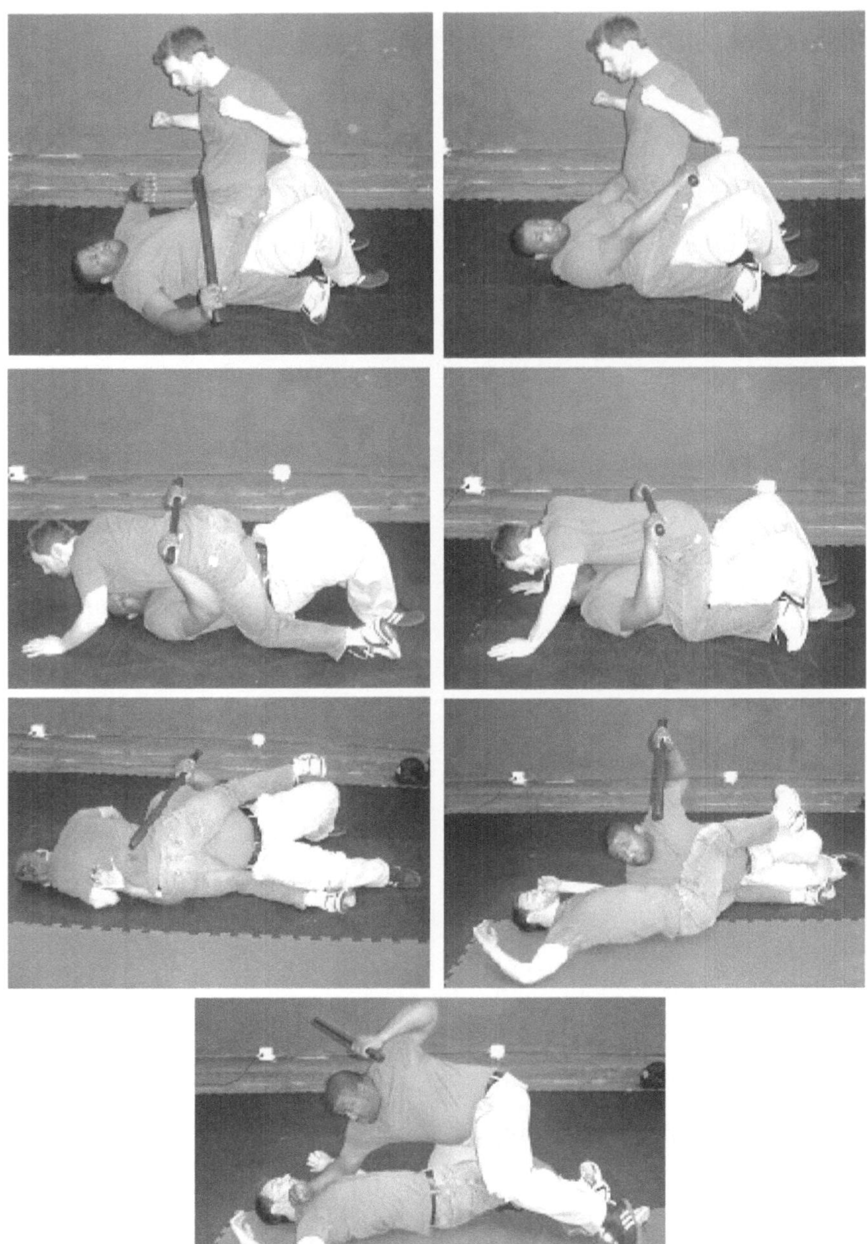

The Warrior finds himself mounted by the subject. The Warrior wraps the baton around the subjects back. The Warrior brings the baton across the subjects shoulder. The Warrior pulls the subject into him towards the ground. The Warrior now raises his hips, further putting the subject off balance. The Warrior now rolls to towards the subject's trapped shoulder, rolling the subject off of the Warrior. The Warrior then assumes a ready position, where he can strike or disengage.

TWO HANDED ANKLE PICK:

Warrior takes his baton and places it behind the assailant's ankle. The Warrior will use their shoulder to apply slow and direct pressure to the thigh or shin or knee. *Note the Warrior keeps his head to the outside of the subject's body. The Warrior monitors the subject's legs to avoid being struck with a kick. The Warrior is now ready to retreat to his feet.

DOUBLE LEG TAKE DOWN

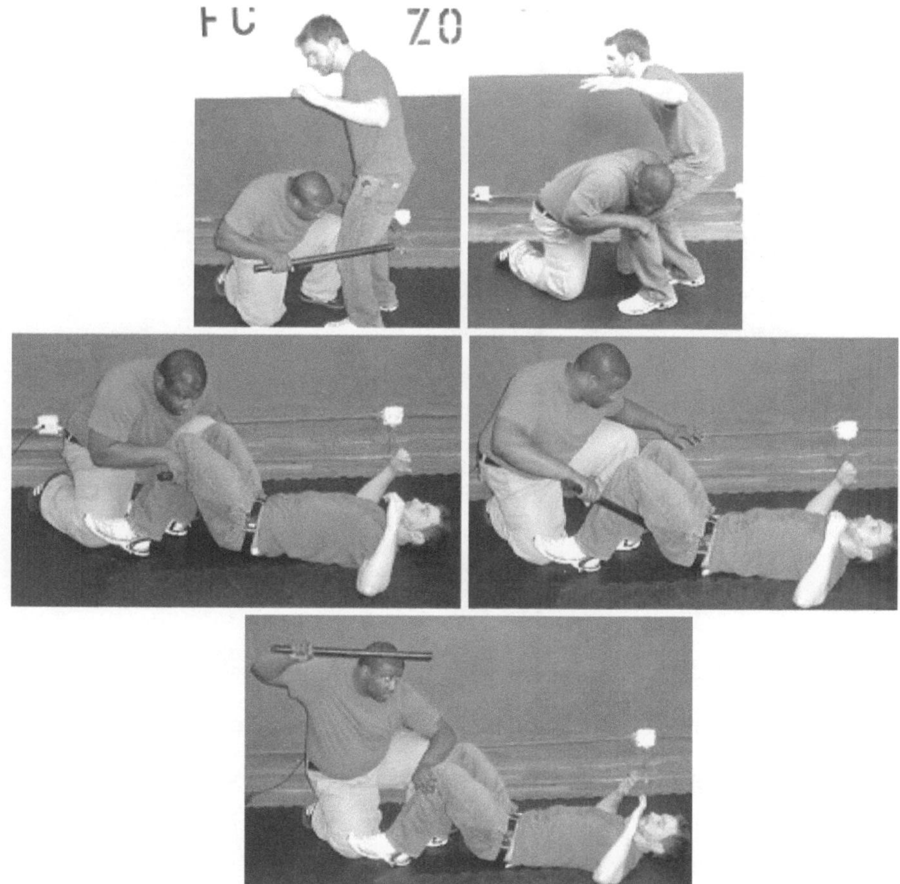

Warrior takes his baton and places it behind the assailant's knees. The Warrior will use their shoulder to apply slow and direct pressure to the thigh or shin or knee. *Note the Warrior keeps his head to the outside of the subject's body. The Warrior releases one end of the baton in order to free it from behind the subject's legs. The Warrior monitors the subject's legs to avoid being struck with a kick. And is now ready to retreat to his feet.

GROUND STRIKING

All of the striking techniques are equally applicable from the various ground positions. The Thrusting strikes presented below are for illustrative purposes.

BIBLIOGRAPHY

1. MCRP 3-02B Close Combat U.S. Marine Corps

2. FM 21-150 Combatives US Army

3. Premiere Martial Arts of Universal City Texas Leadership Manual By Tom & Juanita Howanic

4. Slash & Thrust By John Sanchez

5. Monadnock Defensive Tactics System Manual By Joseph Truncale & Terry E. Smith

6. FMFRP 12-80: Kill or Get Killed U.S. Marine Corps

7. Law Warrior Magazine: Side Handle Batons: What's out there & how to choose By Bob Willis

8. The Evolution of the Police Baton

9. Pro-Systems Baton Manual By Joseph Truncale

10. Cold Steel By John Styers

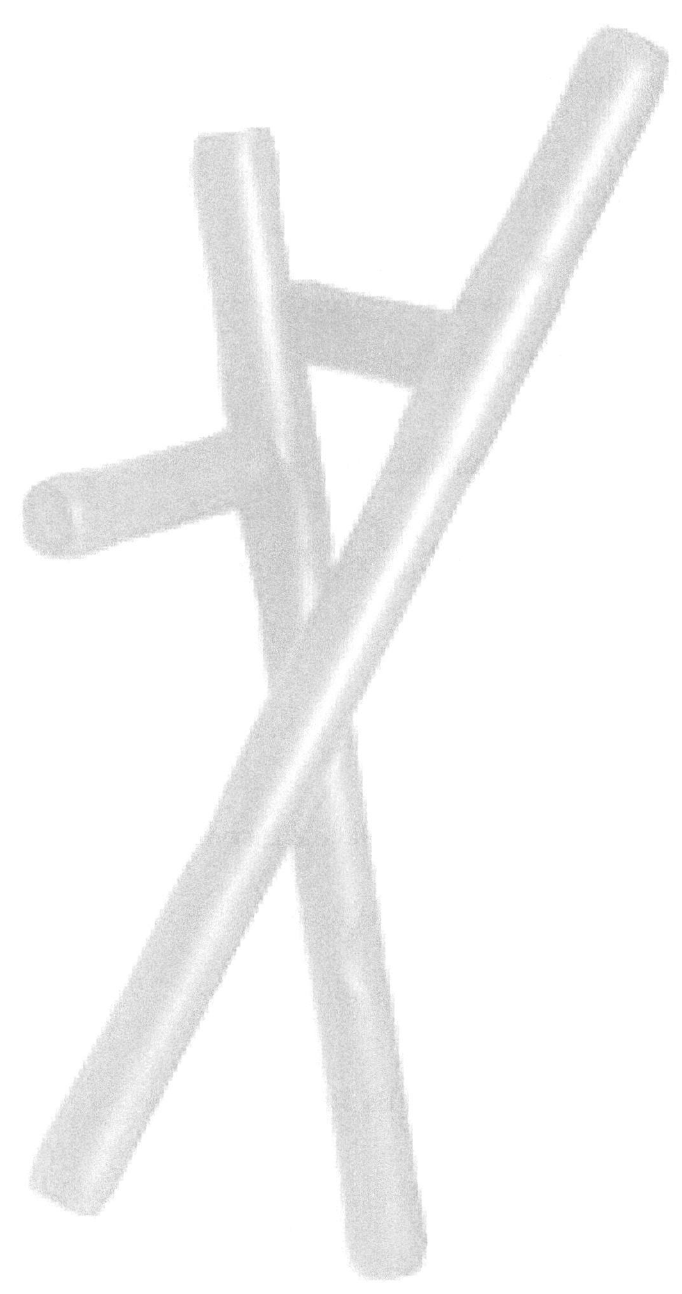

ABOUT THE AUTHOR

Fernan Vargas is the Founder of Raven Tactical International. He has been a student of the Martial Arts for over 30 years. In that Time Mr. Vargas has specialized in the applications of modern and historic combat arts for the purpose of self-protection. Mr. Vargas is a current safety patrol leader and trainer for the Chicago Chapter of the World famous Guardian Angels safety patrol. As a Guardian Angel, Mr. Vargas designed the official defensive tactics program for the organization. As a certified law enforcement trainer Mr. Vargas has taught defensive tactics to law enforcement and security personnel at the local, state and federal level including agencies such as the Pentagon Force Protection Agency, and the Colorado and Virginia Defense Forces. Mr. Vargas has also taught military personnel and civilians in the United States and abroad in countries such as Spain, Italy and Canada. Mr. Vargas holds several instructor credentials in a variety of Impact Weapons including the side handle baton, the expandable baton, the mini baton as well as the martial arts of Bushi Satori Ryu and DFA Kali.

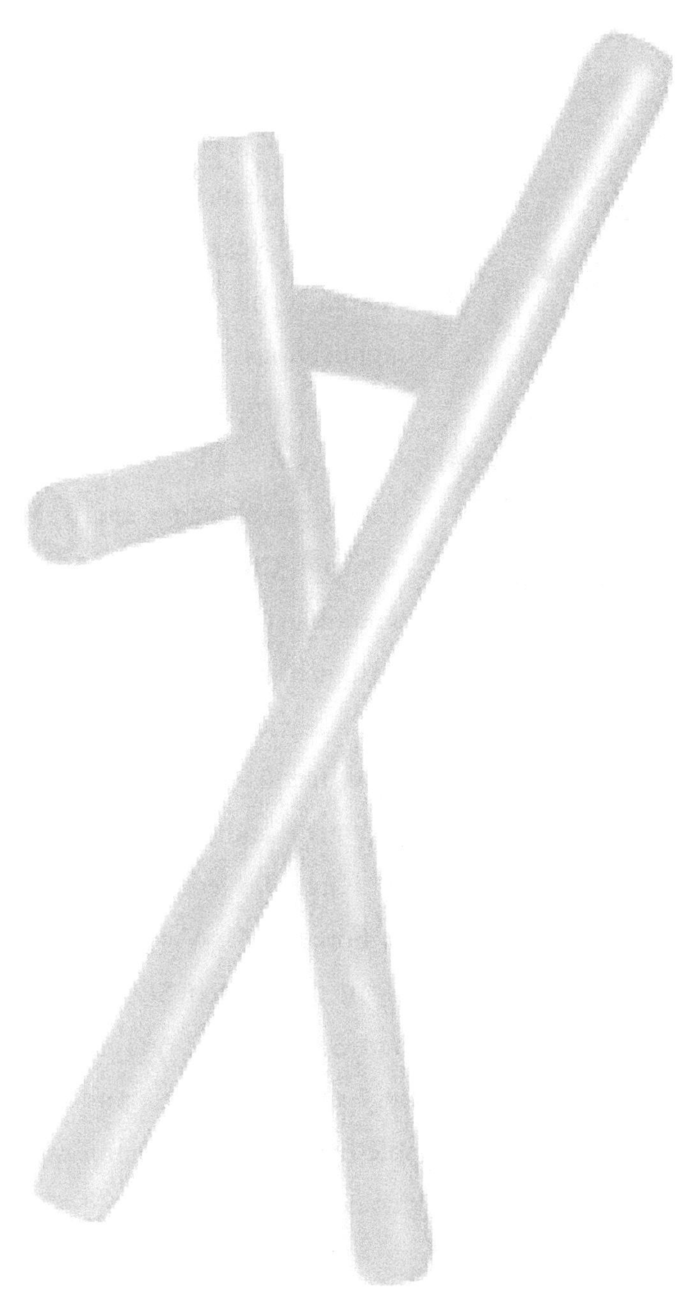

PURCHASE ADDITIONAL BOOKS & E-BOOKS AVAILABLE AT:

WWW.RAVENTACTICAL.COM

WWW.FERNANVARGAS.COM

WWW.THERAVENTRIBE.COM

For additional training in the use of the side handle baton I recommend the following instructors/organizations

Joseph Truncale

www.probushi.yolasite.com

Chad McBroom

www.compfightsys.com

Edward Coello & Maricruz Hernandez
www.kyongcharmoosul.es.tl

James Hogue
www.pukulan.net

Scott McQuaid
www.blacktrianglesilat.com

Tom Howanic
ucpatriotmartialarts.com

David Seiwert
www.dynamicfightingart.com

Larry Smith
www.lawenforcementinstructor.com

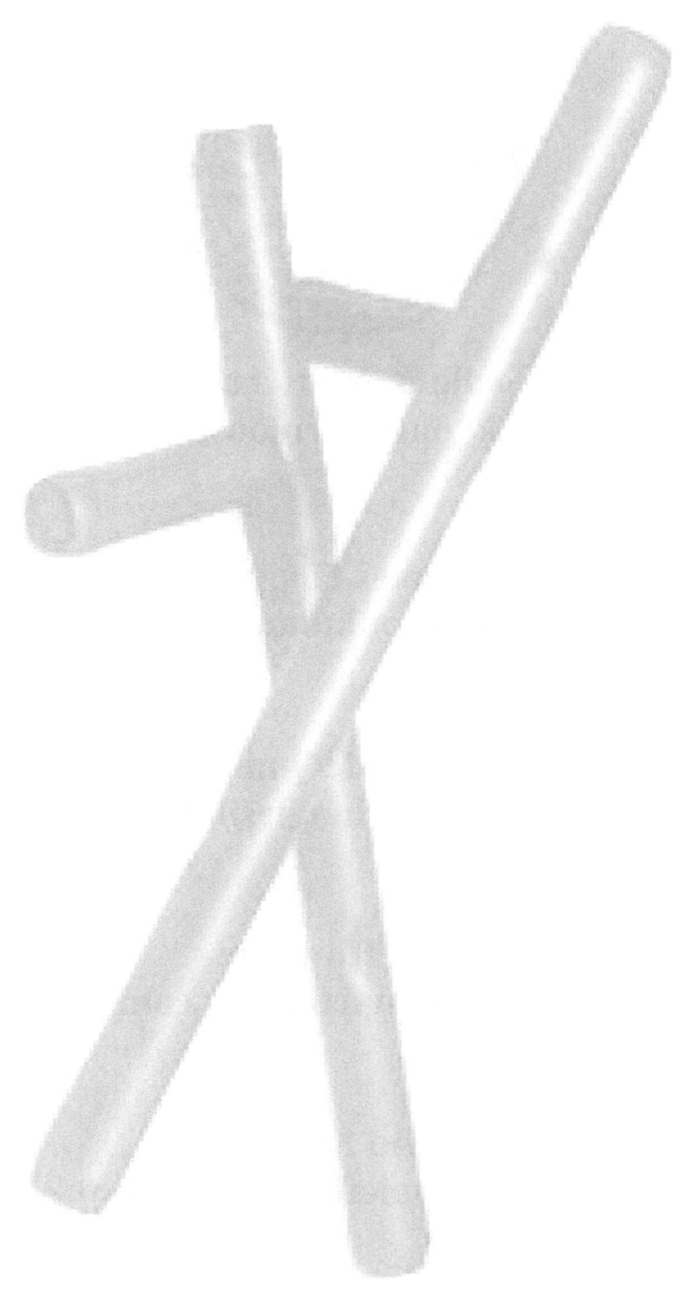

www.ingramcontent.com/pod-product-compliance
Ingram Content Group UK Ltd.
Pitfield, Milton Keynes, MK11 3LW, UK
UKHW041929190726
13854UKWH00004B/1516